DEVON
RAILWAYS

TED   IKE CLEMENT

The
History
Press

Dedicated to all the Railwaymen of Devon

Crowds of sightseers at various points gathered to witness a locomotive that became a legend and a household name: no. 4472 *Flying Scotsman* visited the West Country during October 1963. The image of this engine with steam billowing from its funnel fully captures the romance of the age of steam. The *Flying Scotsman* was exhibited at the British Empire exhibition at Wembley in 1924 and took pride of place in the palace of engineering. Always attracting widespread interest, the locomotive is seen here at Exmouth Junction shed on a rail tour, 19 October 1963.

First published in 1997
This edition published 2009

The History Press
The Mill, Brimscombe Port
Stroud, Gloucestershire, GL5 2QG
www.thehistorypress.co.uk

British Library Cataloguing in Publication Data.
A catalogue record for this book is available from the British Library.

ISBN: 978 0 7524 5213 5

Typesetting and origination by The History Press
Printed in Great Britain

CONTENTS

Littleham station, 4 September 1958, Drummond 0–4–4 tank no. 30676 is running in bunker first with the 11.50 a.m. from Exmouth. Note the Standard class 3 no. 82011 waiting to depart with the 11.32 a.m. from Tipton St John.

Guard Jack Foyle is seen here at Sidmouth station during February 1947 on his last day of service. A heavy snow-fall marked the occasion and Jack Foyle, covered with snow on the left, is seen shaking hands with stationmaster Charles Greening.

INTRODUCTION

The railway was introduced to Devon during the spring of 1844 when the Bristol and Exeter Company completed its line to Exeter. Travelling is more luxurious now than then. The old first-class carriages were tolerable, the second were moderate, and the third were open tubs like cattle wagons, exposed to wind and weather. By 1851 the Devon railway was still confined to the main line from Taunton through Exeter to Plymouth, but over the next fifty years branch lines controlled more often than not by small independent companies reached out through the county.

By the turn of the century the Great Western Railway and the London and South Western covered Devon with only a few small lines remaining independent. The last of these was the Teign Valley which remained in existence until 1923, when the domination of the county by the two great companies was complete.

The coming of the railway contributed much to the development of Devon's seaside towns and for countless generations of holiday-makers Exeter became the gateway to their destination. Before reaching Exeter the Southern Railway travelled via Axminster and Honiton with branch lines pushing down to the seaside resorts of Lyme Regis, Seaton, Sidmouth and Budleigh Salterton through to Exmouth.

Heading down to Plymouth on the old Southern route the train would leave Exeter Central down over the bank and through St Davids tunnel into St Davids station to follow the western line out to Cowley Bridge Junction, the Southern line would then swing back on the left passing stations that all railway men knew by heart, Newton St Cyres, Crediton, Yeoford, Bow, Meldon Quarry, Bridgestowe, Lydford, Brentor, Tavistock North, Bere Alston, Bere Ferrers, Tamerton Folliot Halt, St Budeau Victoria Road, Devonport Kings Road, Devonport Junction and finally 58 miles from Exeter Plymouth North Road.

Two other routes, one to north Devon the other to north Cornwall, were also operated by the Southern Railway. The train for north Devon would leave Yeoford taking the line at Coleford Junction to travel for just over 42 miles via stations like Copplestone, Morchant Road, Lapford, Eggesford, Kings Nympton, Portsmouth Park, Umberleigh, Chapelton, Barnstaple Junction, Barnstaple Town, Pottington, Wrafton, Braunton, Mortehoe and Woolacombe to arrive at Ilfracombe. The trains for north Cornwall would swing away to the left at Meldon Junction passing the Meldon viaduct and climbing to over 900 ft above sea level (the highest point on the Southern Railway system) for the 60-mile journey to the north Cornwall resort of Padstow; extensions from this line went to Holsworthy and Bude giving holiday-makers easy access to the north Devon resorts. The main line of the Great Western Railway from Bristol to Penzance went through Tiverton Junction, Exeter St Davids, Newton Abbot and Plymouth with branch lines to Tiverton and Torbay, the Torbay line reaching as far as Kings Wear. Both lines were efficient and safe to use, men were proud to work on them and passengers who travelled on these railways felt a great affection for what must have been a very environmentally friendly system.

The railway network in Devon was to remain virtually intact until the re-shaping of the British railways or Beeching Report of 1963 which advocated closure of most of the branch lines throughout the country in retrospect. The result was a disaster for Devon.

No book on Devon railways would be complete without a mention of Exmouth Junction engine shed. The original locomotive shed of the London and South Western Railway was at Exeter Queen Street situated just to the east of the station. This depot was here until 1887 when the new engine shed at Exmouth Junction opened on 3 November of that year. Due mainly to poor construction this shed was replaced with a new building completed in 1927.

It was a single shed with the entrance on the west side; 270 ft long by 248 ft wide, it contained twelve roads on shed and one lifting road. A new 65-ft turntable electronically operated coaling plant had a bunker capacity of 200 tons. A hoist would take a 20-ton wagon and lift it 60 ft a minute, the wagon travelling along to the centre and then being turned through an angle of 135 degrees. The average time for coaling an engine was 2½ minutes.

Michael Clement well remembers when he first came to Exmouth Junction shed as a young cleaner in 1952 – he worked a six-day week with four different duty turns. At that time 140 locomotives were allocated to the shed with over 400 men working there. Gangs of cleaners were allocated to clean engines by the charge hand. Michael recalls the welcome break halfway through your duty time to brew up a can of tea from the kettle in the cleaners' cabin, or have a woodbine bought from the timekeeper's office, then have your lunch with perhaps time for a game of cards before being hustled out by the charge hand to clean the next batch of engines or oil some underneaths. After a time young Michael attended a firing class taken by a Mr Edgar Snow, a week at Exeter Central in the class room and a week on the shed at Exmouth Junction. This was followed by the shed master Mr Horace Moore asking him practical questions after which he passed first as a fireman then as a driver.

During the peak summer months Michael found that Exmouth Junction shed was a busy place especially on a Saturday, when the two disposal roads and the coaling plant would be full up. Engines came in and were 'squared up'. This was a term used by enginemen for topping up the boiler with their injectors, cleaning out the smokebox, cleaning the fire, raking out the ashpan and then making

Another picture of Seaton station yard during the summer of 1963. In the background standing in platform two are London coaches; this was to be the last regular summer working of steam on the branch line. The man posing for the camera seen unloading a box wagon for Pioneer Haulage from Beer was Derek Barratt.

up the fire again. They would then take coal and if necessary turn the engine on the turntable, come back on shed and fill up with water. The engine would be ready then bar the fire being pushed out and made up for another trip out. With the 'Black 'uns', 'Woolworths', and Drummond tanks squaring up required the use of fire irons, clinker shovel, dart and pricker, but the West Country packets and the Standard class had rocking bars and ashpans. The Standard had this as well as self-cleaning smokeboxes thus cutting down time on the pits. As well as coming in, engines would be going out to work on trains to Plymouth, north Devon, north Cornwall, Salisbury and Waterloo. They would also work on carriage shunting duties, bank duties and freight duties, engines leaving the shed to travel down to the pointsman's hut.

It is now over thirty years since the shed closed and Exmouth Junction shed along with most of Devon's branch lines belong to a different age and many of the men who worked there have passed on. Michael, then a young fireman, left the railway early in 1965 but he still remembers the tales and idle chatter in the enginemen's cabin, the smell of steam and hot oil, the rattle of fire irons, the hum of the Bulleid generators, the clink of their injectors and the glow from the fire as you made it up. He never did make it to the main line gang, but he was a railwayman and once a railwayman always a railwayman.

During March 1960 the last steam locomotive built for British Railways left the Swindon Works. BR 2–10–0 class 9F no. 92220 was aptly named *Evening Star* and is seen here on 20 September 1964 in the up sidings at Seaton Junction after working a Farewell to Steam railtour.

Exeter Central station, 2 September 1963; not a usual duty for the smaller Pacifics, but on this day Battle of Britain rebuilt Pacific no. 34056 *Croydon* was in charge of the 12.30 p.m. up Atlantic Coast Express, with men of Exmouth Junction main line gang on the footplate.

MAIN LINES

Honiton station during the LSWR days. An unidentified up train leaves the station carrying the usual Plymouth–Exeter–Salisbury–Waterloo head code, two discs straight up and down in the middle of the buffer beam and smoke box.

On route from Yeovil shed to Exmouth Junction shed, GWR 0–4–2 tanks no. 1442 and no. 1450 pause at Axminster station to top up at the water column, Sunday 7 February 1965. Owing to a shortage of diesel multiple units they were covering duties on the Seaton branch.

The passage of the up Devon Belle, hauled by unrebuilt Merchant Navy class no. 35024, *East Asiatic Company*, is watched by the duty signalman and railway staff on the up platform of Axminster station on a wet summer day in 1953. The rain is driving the exhaust down around the express. The four-coach Lyme Regis branch line train stands in the bay platform.

The up Plymouth to Brighton through train heads out of Axminster towards Axminster Gates in September 1959. In charge is West Country class light Pacific no. 34107 *Blandford Forum* with men from Salisbury Shed on the footplate.

Battle of Britain class no. 34065 *Hurricane* thunders under Weycroft bridge going on towards Axminster Gates, summer 1954. The locomotive is heading a down West of England express.

Before the arrival of the Bulleid Merchant Navy and West Country class Pacifics the mainstay for many years on the West of England main line to Exeter were the Urie- and Maunsell-designed King Arthur class locomotives. Here, during September 1959, departing Seaton Junction with a Yeovil to Exeter Central stopping train, is King Arthur class 4–6–0 no. 30451 *Sir Lamorak* from the Salisbury shed.

The special quality of steam is revived in this picture taken on 21 June 1992 from the old down platform on the deserted Seaton Junction. Almost by magic the clock is turned back sixty years to the halcyon days of steam, and here we have a sight charged with interest for all railway enthusiasts. For the first time in twenty-seven years a steam locomotive passes through the junction to tackle the notorious Honiton bank: no. 777 *Sir Lamiel* is the sole survivor of the Southern King Arthur class. With her ten-coach train behind she provided opportunity seldom encountered to sense an age before steam power was replaced by impersonal diesel.

Here, in Michael Clement's favourite photograph, Drummond T9 class 4–4–0 express passenger locomotive no. 705 heading a down West of England express is in full flight out of the west end of Honiton tunnel. This picture, taken on 4 August 1928, shows the train passing the long closed Honiton tunnel west box on the down side. The two boxes were brought into use between January 1899 and May 1902 when work carried out in the tunnel made single line working necessary.

London & South Western railway advertisement, c. 1906.

With safety valves lifting at 200 lb per square inch, S15 class no. 30828 drifts down Honiton bank, summer of 1961. The S15 class engines were known to the men that worked them as 'Black 'uns'. They worked many of the local stopping trains and were also on goods traffic. Standing in the branch siding at Seaton Junction is an unidentified Drummond M7 tank.

Driver Dan Weston and a relief fireman from Exmouth Junction attend to Drummond tank no. 30125, which is standing in the branch platform of Seaton Junction, Saturday 2 June 1962. In the background on the down local road West Country Pacific no. 34107 *Blandford Forum* waits with a train for Exeter Central. Note the main line crew on the footplate looking back to the train for right of way from the guard, and the signalman looking out of the signal box.

Honiton tunnel east end, August 1995. A distance of 78 chains from Honiton incline box, the tunnel is 1,345 yds long. The track is now a single line through the tunnel. While the tunnel was being built a man could look through it and see a pin point of light at the other end. Not until the end of steam could this light be seen again, because the smoke lingered from the trains for such a long time. Even today if you enter the tunnel mouth the smell of sulphur from the brickwork still remains.

West Country class no. 34024 *Tamar Valley* leaves Honiton station with an up local stopping train, 21 July 1958.

A rebuilt West Country class 4–6–2 no. 34037 *Clovelly* heads the 11.45 a.m. Bude to Waterloo towards the west end of Honiton tunnel, 13 August 1962. This fine picture shows how well the permanent way staff kept the railway embankments.

A unique war time photograph showing Merchant Navy class Pacific no. 21C9 *Shaw Saville* descending Honiton bank with a twenty-coach up train loaded with sandbags to the weight of passengers during trials in 1942. These trials took place to assess the locomotives' power and performance and also to test the coal and water consumption. The Merchant Navy class was thirty locomotives, which were named after British and allied shipping lines of the Second World War.

Exeter Central station, 1958. Unrebuilt Merchant Navy Pacific no. 35019 *French Line CGT* with the tail light on the front end has just run light engine from Exmouth Junction shed to Exeter Central ready to work the passenger train up to Waterloo. It now backs on to the passenger train in the platform, and once coupled up the tail light will be removed; the Exeter to Waterloo route discs will then be displayed.

Originality and variety in railway photographs are always welcome and this glimpse into the cab of Merchant Navy Pacific no. 35012 *United States Lines* is worthy of study. She was standing ready for a run to Waterloo: the fire was made up and the boiler pressure was right up on the mark. Note the tray, with the tea can and cup to provide that welcome brew-up.

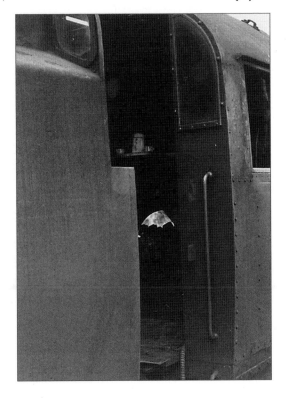

A fine photograph of Sidmouth Junction taken by Roger Joanes, 2 September 1962. He managed to capture an unusual visitor on the West of England main line – Schools class 4–4–0 no. 30925 *Cheltenham* departing with the 11 a.m. Exeter to Waterloo train. It was claimed that 30925 gave the

finest performance of the forty School class engines. Note the tall signal box in this picture directly behind the train on the up side.

Mutley station, Plymouth, *c.* 1909. Plymouth at this time was served by the GWR and LSWR; the former had a terminus at Millbay, rebuilt in 1901, and other stations at North Road and Mutley (pictured here); the two latter were also used by the LSWR whose terminus was at Friary. The stationmaster at Mutley at the time of this photograph was Thomas Arthur.

Okehampton station, May 1959. The town of Okehampton adjoins Dartmoor, and the station was on the main line of the old LSWR. In this picture T9 class no. 30709 is waiting at the station with an Exeter Central to Plymouth stopping train.

A once familiar scene in Exeter Central, which R.C. Riley successfully captured on 23 July 1958. The picture takes us on a trip of nostalgia into the days of steam to see Merchant Navy class 35009 waiting to depart with a train for Waterloo. In the foreground West Country class no. 34106 Lydford stands while E1/R class 0–6–0 tank no. 32135 hurries in with a goods train from Exmouth Junction yard.

The eastern approaches to Exeter Central station were spacious and level with the typical modern Southern layout. During July 1958 West Country class 4–6–2 no. 34035 *Shaftesbury* passes Exeter Central 'A' box with an Exeter to Salisbury local, while Battle of Britain class no. 34056 *Croydon* runs into the south side of the station with a down express. With Exeter Central as its focal point the old London & South Western dominated Devon and a great rivalry existed between it and the Great Western Railway. All this was to change after the nationalization of railways in 1948, and by the time of this picture British Railways had come into being. The passing of the two railway companies at midnight on 31 December 1947 was a sad day for many of the older railwaymen who took great pride in the individuality of their companies. Worse was to follow with the BR modernization plan of 1955 and the Beeching Report of 1963, which resulted in the reduction of route mileage from nearly 20,000 to 12,500 miles.

Coming up St Davids bank (a climb of 1 in 37) and passing Exeter Central 'B' box is Battle of Britain class no. 34069 *Hawkinge* with a train from the west, 21 September 1963. No doubt *Hawkinge* was assisted in the rear by a banker.

West Country class no. 34096 *Trevone* in rebuilt form, seen here at Exeter St Davids with the down Brighton to Plymouth through train, August 1962.

Photographer Derek Cross managed to capture something of the private working world of the railways with this fine period picture taken in July 1958. A stone train with ballast from Meldon Quarry is climbing up the last bit of the ¾ mile curving 1 in 37 bank from Exeter St Davids to Exeter Central. The train, hauled by an N class, has topped the summit with two E1/R 0–6–0 tank engines as bankers bringing up the rear. The limestone and granite quarries at the Meldon were 2½ miles south-west of Okehampton. Meldon Viaduct nearby is a notable piece of railway engineering carrying the railway over a deep ravine of 160 ft.

This exceptional view of Merchant Navy class no. 35003 *Royal Mail* awaiting the right of way from platform three Exeter Central with a train for Waterloo was taken by R.M. Casserley on 28 July 1962.

Merchant Navy class no. 21c2 *Union Castle* in original condition runs into Exeter Central station with an express from Waterloo, 31 August 1945. The photographer, clearly accomplished in his composition of railway pictures, successfully captured the express passing an unidentified M7 Drummond tank in the left-hand corner.

The story of the old Sidmouth branch line is one which will still bring memories flooding back to many railwaymen. It was one of several branches off the main line which are no longer there. Here is British Railways Standard class 2 2–6–2 tank no. 41307 coming slowly off the Sidmouth branch bunker first hauling a pick-up freight on to the main line at Sidmouth Junction in about 1959. Note the fireman keeping a sharp look out from the cab.

The Southern Railway vigorously promoted Devon as a holiday resort and provided trains such as the Devon Belle, seen here on 8 July 1949. The Devon Belle was introduced in June 1947 to run between Waterloo, Plymouth and Ilfracombe. During the early years the Belle was often loaded to fourteen coaches totalling some 550 tons. The train, which ceased running in September 1954, was made up entirely of Pullman cars. In this picture the down Devon Belle passes by the coal hopper at Exmouth Junction shed with unrebuilt Merchant Navy Pacific no. 35007 *Aberdeen Commonwealth* in charge.

T9 4–4–0 no. 30710 at Plymouth, 1950s.

Battle of Britain class no. 34076 with a train from Plymouth via Okehampton, passing Cowley Bridge Junction, 1 September 1962.

The Pullman observation car of the down Devon Belle is seen here on 8 July 1949 passing Exmouth Junction shed, heading into Exeter Central. Note the M7 Drummond tank in the background.

The immaculate composition of this picture clearly shows that C.L. Caddy was an accomplished railway photographer. The notice board (long disappeared) gives the information that this was Sidmouth Junction, where one could change for Ottery St Mary, Tipton St John, Sidmouth and Budleigh Salterton, for example. Here, on 12 September 1964, is an up stone train with ballast from Meldon Quarry, hauled by Standard class 5 no. 73161.

West Country class no. 34033 *Chard* at Honiton station with a down stopping train, 2 September 1959. The new signal box pictured was opened on 16 June 1957 and was situated on the up side.

S15 class no. 30826 departs from Exmouth Junction freight yard with an up freight, 17 July 1962. These engines worked most of the freight traffic between Exeter and Nine Elms and were known by enginemen as 'Black 'Uns'. The Exmouth Junction men who worked these engines were called 'the black gang link'.

BRANCH LINES

S15 class no. 30846 runs into Axminster station during the summer of 1962 at the head of an up stopping train. The Lyme Regis branch train seen in the bay platform is waiting for passengers.

Axminster station, 28 January 1961. The fireman of Adams radial tank no. 30583 had completed his job and made up his fire. With safety valves lifting at 160 lb per square inch, the engine with its one-coach train stands ready for the right of way and the 4 mile stiff climb to Combe Pyne. Note the River Axe in full flood in the background.

A pleasant rural setting on the Southern region, 10 July 1956. Adams tank no. 30582 runs around its branch train at Axminster. In the foreground you can see the well-tended staff allotments, which were to disappear when the Lyme branch line closed.

Adams radial tanks no. 30582 and no. 30584 double head their five-coach train, which was part of the 10.45 a.m. Saturday only from Waterloo, August 1960. The train for Lyme Regis is on the 1 in 40 bank out of Axminster towards Abbey Gate.

Adams tank no. 30584 is climbing up the 1 in 40 bank, summer 1956. Note the Axminster fixed distant signal in the background.

Combpyne station, 8 July 1959. The only intermediate station on the Lyme Regis branch line, Combpyne was 4 miles and 21 chains from Axminster. The station buildings, which are substantial brick-built erections, lie detached beyond the siding. In the background a holiday camping coach is standing against the stop blocks. Locomotive Adams tank no. 30584 with its one-coach train is seen in the foreground underway for Lyme Regis.

This remarkable photograph was taken looking through the cab window on Adams tank no. 30583, giving a driver's eye view to the right of the footplate. The train is climbing up through Combpyne Woods where the oak and beech trees combine with primroses and bluebells in the spring to make a delightful scene.

Combpyne station, Thursday 6 July 1961. Junior porter Mike Clement is on duty and can be seen loading 5 gallon water churns into the two-coach Lyme Regis train. Combpyne station and the station house had no running water or electricity; the water was brought from Lyme Regis in these 5 gallon water churns. The station house was provided with nine churns and the station with a ½ gallon churn. During the summer months water also had to be provided for the camping coach seen in the background. A loading bay for goods was placed centrally on the further side of the platform and station lighting was by means of oil lamp and later tilley lamps.

Seaton station, on the Seaton branch of the London & South Western Railway, 1908. The staff on the main platform are standing beside an Adams D2 class locomotive with the branch train. The stationmaster at that time was Alfred Edward Taylor and the men on the right of the picture worked for Bradford and Sons Ltd, coal and general merchants, who operated from the railway station.

During May 1963 the Drummond M-7 tanks and the Southern pull and push sets were replaced on the Seaton branch line by GWR auto trains. These were worked by 0–6–0 pannier tanks which because of their poor condition were soon replaced by the class 2 Standard tanks. The 0–6–0 pannier tank no. 6412 seen here taking water originally came from Cardiff Canton Shed.

A two-coach diesel unit stands at Seaton platform two waiting to depart for the junction. This photograph was taken during the summer of 1965, the last summer working on the branch line.

Diesel railcars operated on the Seaton branch line from November 1963 until its closure in March 1966. Here we see diesel multiple unit no. W55001 approaching Colyford gates with the 4.45 p.m. from Seaton Junction on 8 May 1964. The driver in charge was Harold Pope.

Colyton station, 7 July 1959. Drummond M7 tank no. 30021 leaves with a train for Seaton Junction.

M7 Drummond tank engine no. 30045 runs bunker first into Colyton station with the 4.47 p.m. from Seaton Junction, 2 September 1959.

Exeter Central platform four, 18 July 1958. Drummond 0–4–4 M7 tank no. 30044 waits to depart for the Exmouth branch line. Exmouth is 10½ miles by rail from Exeter and the journey included stops at Topsham, Woodbury and Lympstone. 4 miles out of Exeter the train would draw up at Topsham and would then travel along the river bank enabling passengers to admire the scenery. At the turn of the century there were about twenty trains daily each way between Exeter and Exmouth, including a special express which left Exmouth in the morning and returned from Exeter in the evening.

Heading for the Exmouth branch line with the 10.45 a.m. for Exmouth, M7 tank no. 30024 passes Exeter Central 'A' box with its five-coach train, 6 July 1957.

Here on 10 July 1962 at Exmouth station a rather scruffy Standard class tank no. 82011 stands at platform three getting ready to leave with a train for Exeter Central, working bunker first. The water tower and engine shed can be seen on the far left.

Like most seaside towns, Budleigh Salterton owes much of its development to the railway. The branch line from Exmouth that ran through Budleigh Salterton on its way to Sidmouth Junction lasted for sixty-four years. In this fine picture of Budleigh Salterton station, taken on 9 July 1959, British Railways Standard class 3 tank no. 82025 has just arrived with the 6.16 p.m. Exmouth to Budleigh service. The locomotive will run around its train and return to Exmouth with the 6.38 p.m.

Photographs of this type and quality typify West Country branch line stations during the 1920s. Here we have Sidmouth station on 4 August 1928, and standing in the station Adams T1 class 0–4–4 tank no. 80 with its three-coach train, the 6.15 p.m. to Sidmouth Junction.

BR Standard class 2–2–6–2 tank no. 41309 leaves Tipton St John station with a branch train for Sidmouth, 27 April 1963.

Running bunker first to Sidmouth Junction, Standard class 3 no. 82025 heads away from the outskirts of Exmouth to cross Exmouth viaduct, 12 October 1959. When the line closed on 6 March 1967 this viaduct was demolished.

Here on the Exeter Central–Exmouth branch on 1 September 1958 is Drummond M7 tank no. 30669 running into Woodbury Road en route to Exmouth. A few days after this photograph was taken Woodbury Road was renamed Exton.

Interested spectators gather to watch the arrival at Sidmouth station of 0–6–0 pannier tank no. 4666 and its three-coach train. Members of a locomotive club were on a rail tour.

Littleham station, a distance of 173 miles 74 chains from Waterloo, 1959. Standard class 2 tank no. 41306 arrives with the 1.30 p.m. from Exmouth, while Drummond M7 tank no. 30024 waits with the 1.14 p.m. from Tipton St John.

Newton Poppleford station, on the branch line of the LSWR from Tipton St John to Budleigh Salterton, 6 September 1958. BR Standard class 3 no. 82010 is seen running into the station with its three-coach train, the 5.35 p.m. from Tipton St John.

A pleasing picture, showing Standard class 3 no. 82011 running bunker first on a mixed train before running into the branch platform at Sidmouth Junction, September 1959.

A good action picture taken by H.B. Priestley, 9 September 1959. The art of exchanging tablets between signalman and fireman on a moving locomotive is clearly shown in this photograph. The signalman offers his tablet up with the fireman holding his down. Practice made perfect, but the secret was to keep your eye on the tablet offered, and to let your arm slip through the loop; the momentum of the locomotive did the rest. The weight of the tablet was approximately 1½ lb, and it was enclosed in a leather pouch with a brass ring on the pouch. When the fireman took the tablet the speed of the train swung the pouch against the side of the engine, with the brass ring hitting the side and protecting the tablet inside. The exchange here took place at Lympstone on the Exeter Central to Exmouth branch, with the fireman of Standard class 3 no. 82013 on the 11.45 a.m. from Exmouth preparing to hand over the Exmouth to Lympstone tablet; he is about to receive the Lympstone to Exton tablet from the signalman.

The development of the steam locomotive during the nineteenth century led to a network of railway lines spreading across the country, giving small resorts such as Budleigh Salterton a new lease of life. The station was on a branch of the LSWR, which joined the Sidmouth branch at Tipton, 6½ miles distant with an intermediate station near Otterton Bridge and East Budleigh. A further line was constructed in 1901 uniting the station with Exmouth. In the picture above Budleigh Salterton station is seen on 8 September 1961; today much of the station is part of Normans supermarket. The picture below, taken on the same day, shows Drummond M7 tank no. 30670 leaving the station with its two-coach train, and entering the steep cutting en route for East Budleigh.

EXETER & BEYOND

The 10.28 a.m. to Waterloo departs Exeter Central station on 6 July 1957. Seen here passing Exeter Central 'A' box the train of thirteen coaches is hauled by immaculate Merchant Navy rebuilt Pacific no. 35023 Holland Afrika Line. *This locomotive was rebuilt in the February of that year.*

Torquay railway station, 1959. This fine press photograph by the *Western Morning News* marks the beginning of the end of steam. Here on a wet day we see the first diesel engine on the Torbay Express.

GWR County class no. 1009 *County of Carmarthen* with its eight-coach train climbs up from Torre, 1950s. The line to Torre was opened to traffic on Monday 18 December 1848 after being opposed by a few of the inhabitants. By the turn of the century there were two stations for the town, one at Torquay and one at Torre, both on the Dartmouth and Torquay branch of the GWR.

Platform four Exeter Central is seen here on 29 September 1956. Drummond M7 tank no. 30669 waits to depart for the Exmouth branch with its three-coach train.

QUEEN St YARD. cvi

Exeter Queen Street east end approaches, before rebuilding in the 1930s.

Exeter Central platform one, 1 July 1961. In a typical railway photograph of this period, British Rail Standard class 3 tank no. 32024 is waiting with a train for the Exmouth branch.

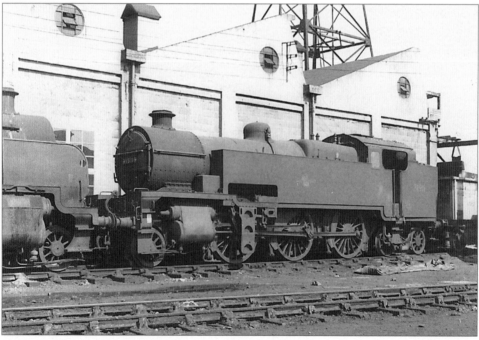

One of Maunsell's W class mixed traffic tank engines no. 31911 is seen here at Exmouth Junction shed on 15 September 1963 in store. This locomotive is standing in what was termed by Exmouth Junction men as the up under the wall road.

The down Atlantic Coast express to Plymouth runs into Okehampton station hauled by West Country class no. 34030 *Watersmeet*, October 1949. The Atlantic Coast express ran daily from 1927 in both directions under the Southern Railway until the end of the summer service in 1964 when the Western Region took over control of the line west of Salisbury. During the height of the summer season the Atlantic Coast express ran in three portions – the Plymouth, the North Devon and the North Cornwall – and was full of holidaymakers.

The Royal Albert Bridge, Saltash, *c.* 1920. One of Brunel's masterpieces of engineering, the Royal Albert Bridge carried the railway over the River Tamar into Cornwall. The bridge, nearly half a mile long, has nineteen spans, the two sides (445 ft) supported by a 35 ft granite pier riding from the bed of the river.

West Country class no. 34002 *Salisbury* climbs up from St Davids to Exeter Central with a passenger train from the west, 29 September 1956.

Z class no. 30955 and an N class 2–6–0 prepare to tackle the 1 in 37 bank from St Davids to Exeter Central with an up freight train from the west, August 1962. The train was probably assisted by a banker at the rear.

The Duke of Cornwall class engines were produced in 1895 by William Dean to work Great Western express trains west of Exeter. Here on an undated picture we have the locomotive *Trefusis*, which belonged to that class.

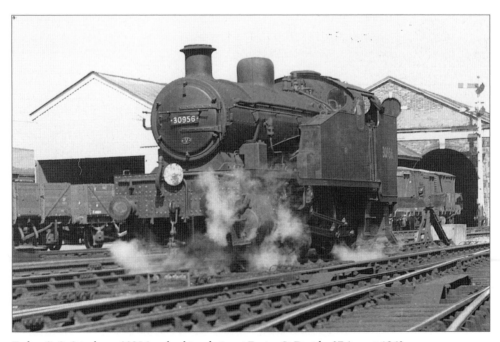

Z class 0–8–0 tank no. 30956 on banking duties at Exeter St Davids, 27 August 1962.

In this picture of considerable interest you can see Drummond mixed traffic engine no. 137 of the K10 class standing on the up side at Exeter Central, 31 August 1945. On the right in the background is the Exeter prison building.

Battle of Britain class no. 34070 *Manston* prepares to leave Exeter Central with the 1.10 p.m. stopping train for Salisbury, 9 September 1963.

LOCOMOTIVES

Merchant Navy Pacific no. 35024 East Asiatic Company has just come off the 9 a.m. from Waterloo at Exeter Central, 9 September 1962. She is pictured here heading back tender first to Exmouth Junction shed where the fire will be cleaned and made up. The engine will also be coaled and watered ready to work the 4.30 p.m. back to Waterloo. For many years the first coach of the 9 a.m. train carried convicts travelling from London via Exeter to Tavistock North station, from where they were convoyed by road to the prison in Prince Town.

Sidmouth Junction, 4 August 1928. The branch line to Sidmouth opened on Monday 6 July 1874. On the first day over a thousand children from Sidmouth, Sidbury and Salcombe Regis headed by the band marched to witness the arrival of the 1.45 p.m. train and the departure of the 2.40 p.m. This was followed by tea, games and sports. During the following week a celebration was given for 400 aged and poor people, with more than a hundred of them given a chance for a ride to Sidmouth Junction and back. The Junction stood in the village of Feniton and at the time of this picture was a busy place. Firms like Miller and Lilley operated from the station, and even W.H. Smith & Son had a place there. In recent years an increasing interest in the preservation and use of steam locomotives has been bringing them to more general attention, and we must be grateful to men like H.C. Casserley who had the vision to record engines like the S15 class no. 831 seen here on a mixed traffic train at the Junction sixty-eight years ago.

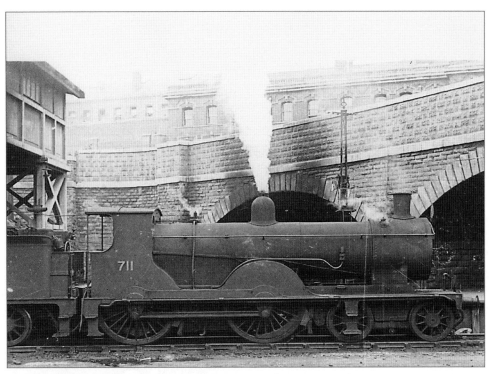

Drummond T9 class 4–4–0 no. 711 seen at Exeter Central, 8 August 1945.

Exeter Queen Street station in the days of the Southern Railway. Looking east in the down through road stands an N class 2–6–0 mixed traffic engine and two Drummond 4–4–0 T9 class engines. In the up through road stands an unidentified tank engine with train.

Battle of Britain class no. 34054 *Lord Beaverbrook* waiting at Sidmouth Junction, May 1956. The locomotive is on an up ballast train from Meldon Quarries; these trains were referred to by railwaymen as stone trains.

During the days of the Southern Railway, West Country class no. 21C113 *Okehampton* waits at Sidmouth Junction on an up express, August 1946. No. 21C113 *Okehampton* had not yet received her name plates, the naming ceremony not taking place until 12 June 1947.

Whimple station, 21 July 1958. S15 class no. 30824 looks really immaculate. Note the shunter in the background.

West Country class no. 214c114 *Budleigh Salterton* at Wadebridge on the north Cornwall line, 7 July 1949.

The Okehampton to Surbiton car carrier heads towards the Black Boy tunnel on 3 August 1963. In charge is Merchant Navy class no. 35016 *Elders Fyffes*.

Another fine railway picture taken by W.L. Underhay, showing West Country class no. 34020 *Seaton* just about to enter the gloom of the 263 yd long Black Boy tunnel at Exeter, heading the 4.42 p.m. Exeter Central to Salisbury train, 3 August 1963.

The two-coach train of the 6.50 p.m. Axminster to Lyme Regis passes under the road bridge at Hartgrove Farm, 1 August 1959. Adams radial tank no. 30584 was built by Dubs and Co., Glasgow, in 1885 and commenced working on the Lyme Regis branch line in 1916. This locomotive was successively numbered 520, 0520, 3520 and 30584, and continued to work the Lyme Regis branch line under the last quoted number until 1961. This locomotive's depot was at Exmouth Junction; while on duty on the branch line it was kept at the Lyme Regis shed.

During the night of 1 October 1960 torrential rain caused severe flooding in the West Country. On Honiton incline, the 5 mile track between Seaton Junction and Honiton, there were more than thirty earthslips at three places; rails were buried for stretches of 30 to 40 yds in 4 to 5 ft of mud. Pictured here is the 1.15 a.m. newspaper train from Waterloo hauled by rebuilt Merchant Navy class no. 35030 *Elder Dempster Lines*. This locomotive ploughed into the first slip and stuck. After carrying out the necessary safety procedures the train was eventually reversed back to Seaton Junction. Note the front end of the engine covered in mud and roots.

Axminster station, 2.30 p.m., 1 March 1956. On the up main line S15 class mixed traffic engine no. 30842 is shunting a goods train. In the bay platform Adams tank no. 30583 has just paid a visit to the coal stage. The late turn Lyme Regis crew seen here are driver George Johns and fireman Grenville Morgan standing by no. 30583.

Pictured here during the summer of 1959 at Axminster station on the Lyme Regis branch bay platform, driver George Johns is bringing back the Adams radial tank no. 30582 and its one coach ready for the trip to Lyme.

Standard class 3 no. 82018 has left Sidmouth Junction and swings off the main line on to the Sidmouth branch with its two-coach train, September 1959. The disc on the engine shows the code for the Sidmouth branch.

Sidmouth Junction, 11 May 1963. Battle of Britain class no. 34065 runs in with the 12.36 p.m. Salisbury to Exeter stopping train. A Standard class 4 2–6–4 tank of the 80000 class can be seen waiting in the branch platform. These engines were very popular with the engine men who worked them.

The naming ceremony of West Country class 4–6–2 Pacific no. 21c120 took place at Seaton Junction on 24 June 1946. The locomotive is seen here in the up station because weight restrictions would not allow West Country Pacifics over the branch line.

West Country class Pacific no. 21c110 *Sidmouth*, 27 June 1946.

Here we see the early morning goods train for Lyme Regis, which had stopped at Combpyne to pick up permanent way lengthman Arthur Watson during June 1961. With Arthur safe in the guard's van Standard class 2 2–6–2 tank no. 41307 is now on its way to Lyme Regis.

Adams 4–4–2 radial tank no. 30520 standing in the up main line at Axminster station, June 1934. The engine is sporting its new Southern Railway livery of SR green with yellow bands and lines and black outlines.

During the summer of 1953 one of the South Western Railway Greyhounds, 4–4–0 T9 class no. 30711, built by Dugald Drummond, arrived at Axminster station with an RCTS special and is seen here awaiting the right of way on the down road.

A photograph taken at Axminster in the late 1950s shows S15 class no. 30847 arriving with a down local from Templecombe to Exeter Central. The locomotive is seen keeping company with Adams tank no. 30584, which was engaged on light shunting duties before taking the branch line train to Lyme Regis.

West Country class no. 34100 *Appledore* passes through Broadclyst station in charge of an up goods train from Exmouth Junction yard, 12 September 1964.

Exmouth station, 12 October 1958. The railway reached Exmouth in 1861 and during the first five days 10,000 people travelled on the line. In 1926 the station was rebuilt and by the 1950s the number of tickets collected at Exmouth was almost as many as those at Exeter Central. In this picture the fine layout of Exmouth station with platforms one to four is plainly shown. In platform three Standard class 3 no. 82017 departs with a train for Exeter Central, and there is empty stock in platform one. On the far left in front of the church spire are the water tank and engine shed of Exmouth locomotive depot.

Smiles all round as Exmouth Junction men pose for this photograph, 22 August 1950. Fireman Dickie Bird is seen standing on the water tank of class E1/R 0–6–2 tank no. 2697; on the left holding an oil can is driver Ted Perkins; next to him is an Exmouth Junction shunter.

Owing to a shortage of diesel units a welcome return to steam took place on the Seaton branch. Here on 27 February 1965 0–6–0 Western tank no. 1442 runs into Colyton station with its one-coach train from Seaton Junction.

Pinhoe station, 14 November 1963. The station is 168 miles 44 chains from Waterloo. In a picture with a period look that attracts immediate interest we see West Country class no. 34023 *Blackmore Vale* leaving with the 1.10 p.m. Exeter Central to Salisbury stopping train.

Sidmouth Junction, September 1959. S15 class no. 30831 pulls away an up stopping train, and in the branch platform Standard class 3 no. 82011 waits to leave with a train for Sidmouth.

Tipton St John, a hamlet on the River Otter, has a station on the Sidmouth branch of the LSWR – which is also the junction for the Tipton St John and Budleigh Salterton branch line. In this picture, taken on 16 August 1960, Drummond M7 tank no. 30024 waits with its two-coach train, the 5.10 p.m. Sidmouth Junction to Sidmouth service.

Sidmouth station, c. 1964. Diesel multiple units were introduced on this branch line on 4 November 1963 and ran until the branch closed on 6 March 1967. Speed restrictions also came into force, of 50 mph between Sidmouth Junction and Tipton St John, and 40 mph between Tipton St John and Sidmouth.

Having worked the Atlantic coast express down from Waterloo, unrebuilt Merchant Navy class no. 35024 *East Asiatic Company*, with two engines behind, stands on the disposal road at Exmouth Junction shed. During the locomotive's visit to Exmouth Junction shed the fire would have been cleaned and made up, and smokebox and ashpan cleaned. It would then be recoaled and watered to be turned on the table ready for a run back to Waterloo. The two route discs on the front indicate Exeter Central and Exmouth Junction.

Exmouth Junction shed, 18 July 1925. The engine pictured here was originally Drummond 4–6–0 no. E333 of the F13 class. In 1924 the engine was withdrawn and laid aside during July and August for rebuilding as a Urie H15 class 4–6–0 mixed traffic engine, no. 30333. This locomotive was finally withdrawn from service in October 1958 having completed a mileage of 1,064,166 miles.

Exmouth Junction shed, 5 July 1957. Waiting to depart light engine for Exeter Central to work the 12.30 p.m. up Atlantic Coast Express is Merchant Navy class no. 35023 *Holland Afrika Line*. Standing beside the locomotive is driver Jack Taylor and looking out of the cab is his fireman George Lawrence; both were from Exmouth Junction's main line gang link. The Merchant Navies totalled thirty in the class and were always known as Packets by the enginemen who worked them. In the background of this picture is Drummond T9 no. 30712.

Exmouth Junction shed, 15 September 1963. Battle of Britain class no. 34083 *605 Squadron*

STATIONS & SIGNAL BOXES

The London & South Western railway reached Exeter in 1860 with a new station under Northernhay in Queen Street. The years that followed became a period of competition between the London & South Western and Great Western Railway, who had their station in St Davids. With both lines passing through the city the advantages to Exeter were many, and for generations of holidaymakers Exeter became the gateway to Devon. Queen Street station, seen here in 1913, was rebuilt in 1933 and renamed Exeter Central.

Broadclyst station, 12 September 1964. West Country class no. 34015 *Exmouth* waits with an up stopping train.

The signalman of the Whimple signal box takes a quiet five-minute break and an opportunist photographer recognizes a good picture, 25 June 1964. The signal box at Whimple was situated on the down platform edge and was 162 miles 79 chains from Waterloo. The box was closed on 11 June 1967.

Tipton St John on the Sidmouth branch of the LSWR, early twentieth century. The stationmaster at this time was Charles Greening. The landlord of the Golden Lion Inn seen on the right was Arthur William Fry.

This excellent railway picture, full of much detailed information, was taken by R.C. Riley on 3 October 1959. Standard class 43 no. 82013 is running into Sidmouth station with its two-coach train; this, combined with the signalman's arm raised waiting to take the Tipton St John to Sidmouth tablet, creates a fine photograph. An extra bonus is the twenty-three lever signal box in the background.

Littleham, once a small struggling village on the coast 2 miles east from Exmouth railway station, became famous as the place where Viscountess Nelson was buried. She became estranged from Lord Nelson when he became involved with Lady Hamilton. She died in 1831 in London and was brought here to Littleham church for burial. Littleham station, on the Exmouth to Sidmouth Junction line, is seen here on 26 September 1966. The building is unusual because the left-hand side was occupied by the ticket office, with the right-hand side serving as the signal box. The line closed on 6 March 1967.

Permanent way men pose for this undated photograph of Littleham, although to judge by their attire it would appear to have been taken during the early part of the twentieth century. A three-coach train from Exmouth is in the station with a locomotive that looks like a Terrier tank, but again this is open to debate.

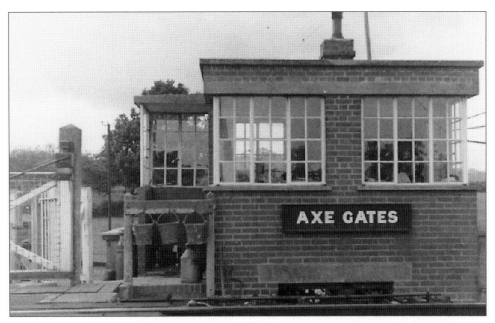

Axe Gates, 141 miles 56 chains from Waterloo, 17 September 1964. Axe Gates had a cottage but unlike Broom Gates (42 chains to the east) and Axminster Gates (2 miles 66 chains to the west) this cottage was demolished when the level crossing gates and box were closed on 6 August 1967. Automatic half barriers were brought into use on 20 August 1967.

Broom Gates signal box, 3 August 1957. Broom Gates, on the main line from Waterloo, could be a busy place to work during the peak summer periods. On Saturdays during the summers of the 1950s railwaymen on early duty from 6 a.m. to 2 p.m. would count through over sixty trains. The crossing gates and box at Broom were closed on 28 August 1967, and automatic half barriers installed.

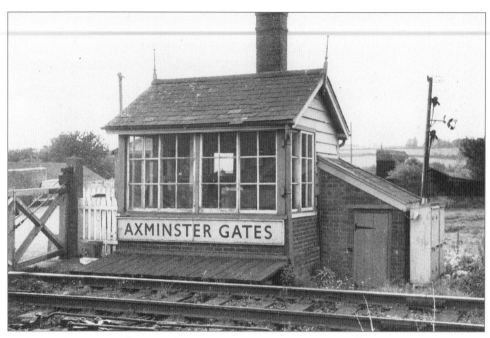

Axminster Gates crossing box, *c.* 1962.

Pinhoe signal box, seen here on 8 July 1959, was a typical small London & South Western signal box with sliding window frame, brick chimney-stack and name board.

Crannaford Gates signal box, 5 March 1966. This was typical of Southern manned level crossings. A cottage was provided for the crossing keeper beside the gates. The gates were removed on 5 March 1966 and automatic half barriers introduced.

The old LSWR and Southern Railway signs at Crannaford Gates; the crossing keeper's cottage can just be seen in the background. Signs like this became targets for souvenir hunters, and nearly all posts that displayed them were stripped.

Broadclyst railway station was 1½ miles south-east of the village on the main line of the London & South Western Railway, 166 miles 57 chains from Waterloo. Situated on the up side was a civil engineers' depot, which was opened by the LSWR in 1896 and extended in September 1929; it was closed down by Western Region in 1964. The photograph above shows the eastern side of the station on 8 July 1957, and the one below is the signal box situated on the up side east of the station taken the same day.

Seaton station, *c.* 1957. The opening in March 1868 of the Seaton branch line of the L & SWR marked a big step forward in the history of the town. The journey from Seaton Junction down the 4 miles to Seaton passed Colyton and Colyford, following the valley of the Axe, to stop just short of the sea. The station seen here was rebuilt in 1936 and demolished after the branch closure in 1966. Before the First World War the first daily train left Seaton station at 7.10 a.m. and the last one arrived at 9.50 p.m. The taxis seen here waiting at the station belonged to Clapps Transport. At the turn of the century there were four bus and coach operators in Seaton using horses, but by 1908 Thomas Clapp had bought up these concerns and continued to offer this service right up to the last day of the railway.

Inside the signal box at Seaton Junction, 1962. The box clock shows the time as 12 noon and signalman Arthur Love is on late turn duty. When he retired from the railway in the mid-1960s Arthur Love had completed over forty-five years' service.

This excellent view of Honiton incline box was taken by W. Phillip Connoly in the 1950s. Here we have a possibly unique picture showing the various instruments for Seaton Junction and Honiton with the ten-lever Stevens frame. This would have read as follows: 1. Down distant, 2. Down Stop signal, 3. Down starter signal, 4. Spare, 5. Cross over road points, 6. Sidings catch points, 7. Cross over and locking bar, 8. Up starting signal, 9. Up stop signal, 10. Up distant. The oil lamp in the window was the only method of lighting in the box.

Gosford Gates, 6 October 1964. Situated 1 mile 39 chains from Sidmouth Junction on the Sidmouth branch line, Gosford Gates was the first of the manned crossings on that line. In the picture above the crossing is shown with the gates across the line with two signals for either direction protecting the gates. In the picture below the crossing keeper's cottage, the water butt on the corner, the railway telephone box and the five-lever Westinghouse frame can be seen.

Standard class 3 tank no. 82025 is pictured here in splendid condition at Budleigh Salterton station, 3 July 1959. The locomotive is just backing on to its train ready to work the 6.30 p.m. service to Exmouth.

Broadclyst station, 8 July 1959. This station, on the main line of the Southern Region railway, was 1½ miles south-east of the village of Broadclyst and 166 miles 57 chains from Waterloo. Following the Beeching Report, Broadclyst station closed on 7 March 1966.

Newton Poppleford station, 7 July 1959. To the layman this country station was little different from many others to be found all over the country, but to the people of Newton Poppleford the opening of this station on the Sidmouth Junction to Exmouth branch line brought great changes and great improvements, providing a service for over sixty-four years. The station and the bridge were demolished after the Beeching purge, and nothing remains today.

East Budleigh station, c. 1960. East Budleigh station was on the Tipton St John to Exmouth line and was 168 miles 41 chains from Waterloo. Looking down the line one can see the goods shed and siding, with the station nameboard and the whitewashed stones reading East Budleigh for Ladram Bay opposite.

Polsoe Bridge Halt was 32 chains from Exmouth Junction. It opened on 31 May 1908 and here Standard class no. 82013 waits with the 11.45 a.m. from Exmouth, 2 September 1959. Michael Clement well remembers when he was a cleaner lad at Exmouth Junction shed, over thirty-five years ago, being told to take dispatch pouches down to the locomotive office at Exeter Central. If no light engine was leaving Exmouth Junction to Central station he would run down to Polsoe Bridge to catch the Exmouth branch train into Central, deliver the pouches and catch the next Exmouth branch train back. For a young cleaner this must have provided a welcome break.

Sidmouth Junction station, looking west towards Exeter. Note the level crossing gates in the distance. This was the junction for Sidmouth branch and also the Exmouth branch, which went via Tipton St John and Budleigh Salterton. Sidmouth Junction was 159 miles and 22 chains from Waterloo.

Honiton station, 21 July 1958.

Lions Holt Halt, pictured here during July 1928, was renamed St James Park on 7 October 1946. Originally opened in 1906, it was used by Exeter City football followers attending matches at St James Park; the football stand can be seen at the top of the bank.

The opening in March 1868 of the branch line of the L & SWR from Colyton Junction (as it was first called) marked a big step forward for the East Devon area. Colyton Junction soon became Seaton Junction and the station buildings are pictured here in 1961. Note the doorway entrance to the booking office and the stationmaster's house on the far side. The station at Seaton Junction was closed on 5 March 1966.

A nostalgic picture of Seaton Junction signal box, 1961. The box was situated on the west end of the down platform, with the Seaton branch running out behind it.

Cadhay Gates, near Ottery St Mary. The name Cadhay dates back to Saxon times, when the land here was occupied by a thane called Cada. In the photograph above Cadhay Gates are seen at the turn of the century, some thirty years after the Sidmouth branch was opened. They were situated on the 2 mile mark from Sidmouth Junction, and were 78 chains from Ottery St Mary. In the picture below, taken on 6 October 1964, the crossing keeper's cottage is shown. An additional hut with a chimney is on the higher side of the cottage, with a 5 gallon water church next to it. Note the telephone fitted to the centre of the cottage and the five-lever Westinghouse frame.

This picture of Axminster station was taken looking up to Axminster Gates in 1961. The station lay to the south-west of the town centre on the old L & SWR route from Waterloo to Exeter. The station platforms were connected by a covered footbridge. The station, which opened on 19 July 1860, is 27 chains from Axminster gates and 144 miles and 66 chains from Waterloo.

The goods shed and sidings of Whimple, 25 June 1954. Whimple station was on the main line of the LSWR, and at the time of this picture the village was still the home of Whiteways Cyder. This firm, which was founded by Henry Whiteway towards the end of the nineteenth century, had its head office and works next to the railway station, and convenient local services operated between Honiton and Axminster to enable employees to travel to work. Season tickets were issued to staff using the railway. During the war years and the immediate post-war period goods were distributed almost exclusively by rail, but by the 1950s the company had built up a lorry fleet and the use of rail freight declined.

Ottery St Mary station, 21 September 1963. The branch line to Sidmouth that served Ottery St Mary opened in 1874, and was closed following the Beeching Report in 1967. Here in this image we have a reminder of a vanished age.

The up platform of Pinhoe station, 8 July 1959. Points of interest are the starting signal, the level crossing gates and signal box. Pinhoe, at one time a pleasant village some 2½ miles north-east of Exeter, had a station on the main line of the London & South Western Railway. This closed on 7 March 1966, but has since re-opened.

A good interior view of the ten-lever frame at Axminster Gates box, which stood at the bottom of Castle Hill, Axminster. Gates like this were manned night and day by the crossing keeper, who more often than not was assisted by his wife.

The uniform of the signalman looking out of the signal box in this undated photograph is either LSWR or SR, which means it was taken pre-1947, before British Rail came into being.

The rather attractive station of Ottery St Mary, 6 October 1964. It served the town well until it was closed to goods and passengers in 1967.

Salisbury

STAFF

A delightful picture taken at Colyford station during the early 1960s. Porter Cyril Welch stands in front of the crossing gates, which were open to main road traffic, to have his photograph taken with two young boys who were enjoying a holiday in East Devon. Because of a back injury in the 1950s Cyril Welch transferred from the permanent way department to the traffic department with light duties at Colyford.

Fireman Harry Park is seen here by the footplate of Drummond M7 tank no. 30045 on platform two at Seaton station, 3 July 1960. Standing on the platform is driver Harold Pope.

Stationmaster Reg Sheppard on duty at Axminster station, 23 November 1957.

Seaton station yard during the days of the Southern Railway. Porter Maurice Phare is seen taking a short rest after dealing with a racing pigeon special train. Seaton was a favourite release point for racing pigeons during the summer months and thousands would be released on Saturdays. Trains of up to fifteen vans would be taken out empty to the junction.

During the years leading up to the Second World War, M. Tregaskis was the local railway agent for Seaton and Axmouth. One of his lorries is seen here in Seaton station yard with driver Maurice Jones standing in front. Southern Railway man Frankie Long is stood at the rear with Arthur Daniels on the back of the lorry.

Not much would escape the eagle eye of stationmaster Maurice Phare, seen here at Axminster station on 19 September 1964.

Pictured here outside their railway cottages in Woodmead Road, Axminster, are three retired Southern Railwaymen, c. 1972. Left to right: Roy Fragel, relief signalman, forty-three years' service; Victor Greenslade, forty years' service with the permanent way department; Valentine Enticott, a signalman with forty-four years' service, many of which were at the Axminster box – he was given this Christian name by his parents because he was born on 14 February, St Valentine's Day. Between them they had served the Southern Railway loyally for over 120 years.

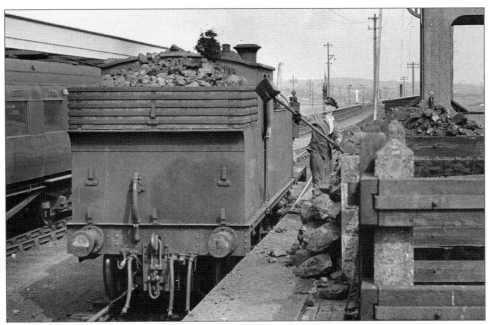

Michael Clement left the traffic department and Combpyne station in January 1962 to join the motive power department at Exmouth Junction shed as an engine cleaner. Returning to Seaton Junction in April 1962 he soon passed for pull and push working, and is seen here on 1 September 1962 on the coaling stage topping up the bunker on M7 tank no. 30045. When this picture was taken Michael was sixteen days short of his seventeenth birthday.

The station yard at Seaton, summer 1963. Workers from Bradford Coal Merchants are loading coal bags on to a Thames Trader lorry. Standing, left to right, Fred Hawker, Charlie Chapple. On the rear of the lorry is Claude Parker.

Situated 141 miles 14 chains from Waterloo, the crossing box at Broom Gates, seen here on 18 July 1964, was the first location in Devon on the Southern Railway. On duty that day and standing by the box is signalman Fred Cook, who came from Axminster.

Station staff at Seaton Junction, *c.* 1926; the station was rebuilt and reopened in 1928. Left to right: Ted Evans (stationmaster), Harry Holmes, Billy Matthews, Arthur Causley, Cyril Barnes, Arthur Love, Alfie Knight. Arthur Causley finished up as the last stationmaster on the Lyme Regis branch line before closure.

Signalman Harry Osmond at Axminster gates signal box, 18 October 1967. The crossing gates were in Castle Hill.

Signalman Lionel Read looking carefree at the same gates, 30 May 1972.

Junior porter Alan Darke at Combpyne station, *c.* 1955. Alan Darke commenced his railway career at Axminster station from where he was transferred to Combpyne. During his time at Combpyne he cycled to work from his home at Uplyme. In 1956 he was called up for national service and on his return to civvy life in 1958 returned to work for the railway at Axminster station. From Axminster he went to Colyton station, where he remained till the closure of the Seaton branch line in 1966.

Stationmaster Harry Wood at Axminster station,
18 December 1956.

The pride of achievement was shown in the
face of Axminster stationmaster Joe Grayer
when this photograph was taken on 12 March
1952. Note his Southern Railway hat and the
pocket watch with chain displayed over his
waistcoat.

Seaton Junction, *c*. 1942. The station staff have posed for this war time photograph, and are standing behind the signal box on the branch platform. These were the days of the old Southern Railway. Back row, left to right: Harry Newton, guard; Arthur Love, signalman; Tony Brooks, leading porter; Raymond Wood, porter; Bernard Pearce, stationmaster. Front row: Don Matthews, leading porter; Jack Warren, signalman; Charlie Beer, porter.

Inside the driving compartment on the two-coach pull and push set on the Seaton branch with driver Dan Weston at the controls. The pull and push system was worked by compressed air with a pump and reservoir on the M7 locomotive; air pipes were fitted to the locomotive and coaches for this system with the normal vacuum brake. An electric bell code operated between the driver in the compartment and the fireman on the footplate.

Running foreman Raymond Down worked at Exmouth Junction shed; he is seen here on 25 April 1963. The shed closed on 6 March 1967, ending an era that had lasted sixty years. There were many happy memories for railwaymen like Mr Down and the countless others who had worked there.

Engaged on shunting duties at Exmouth Junction yard are driver Ted Perkins (left) and fireman Dickie Bird (right), 22 August 1950.

Signalman Grenville Newton worked at the Honiton incline signal box from June 1954 to December 1964. During the 1950s his opposite number was signalman Derek Ostler. Both men went to work on motorcycles: to get to the signal box they had to turn up Hayne Lane in Wilmington, pass under a railway bridge, go through a gate which led to a long pathway to four railway cottages, then go up to the top of the railway bank to ride a few hundred yards beside the track before finally reaching the box.

Situated on the up side at a measured 151 miles 47 chains from Waterloo and 4 miles 4 chains from Seaton Junction stands the Honiton incline signal box, the most lonely box on the Salisbury to Exeter southern main line. The box guarded a 'refuge' siding on the down side with catch points. Goods trains hauling up the bank could use this refuge siding to split their train in times of difficulties. Signalman Harry Osmond is on duty at the box, *c.* 1932.

Signalman Bill Woolaghin on duty at the
Axminster box, *c.* 1962.

Signalman Dick Weller is on duty in the
Axminster Gates crossing box, *c.* 1963.

The branch platform at Seaton Junction, 3 October 1960. Left to right: a relief fireman from Exmouth Junction's junior spare gang link and driver Dan Watson of Seaton.

Driver George Johns with young Exmouth Junction fireman George Knight are pictured together on the Adams radial tank at Axminster station during the 1950s. Note the water tower in the background. A steam engine used to power a pump bringing water from the nearby River Axe.

The BR modernization plan of 1955 and the Beeching Report of 1963 resulted in the phasing out of steam traction during the late 1960s. This picture shows the end of an era when during the evening of 4 November 1963 driver Tom Woodman gets the brake on a Standard class 2 tank no. 41320 at Axminster station, with not only the last train of the day for Lyme Regis but also the last regular steam locomotive to work on the branch line. The class 2 tank took over from the Adams tanks in 1961 and were replaced by diesel units.

Driver Tom Woodman from Uplyme is pictured at the controls of no. 41307, *c.* 1962. He was the driver in charge of the Lyme Regis depot. Tom is wearing on his cap one of the old brass engineman's SR badges issued by the Southern Railway: a fireman had to have so many firing turns to his credit before being issued with one of these. They were replaced by a BR badge in Southern green after nationalization. No doubt pride in his connection with the old Southern Railway was one good reason for Tom Woodman still wearing this cup badge.

Traffic department staff at Axminster station, 15 June 1957. Left, Mr White and right, porter Jim Lilley.

A typical picture of driver Harold Pope with his roll-up cigarette taken in the driving compartment of the two-coach pull and push set after its arrival at Seaton, *c.* 1960. Before leaving the junction for Seaton the air pump would be started on the engine, the regulator would be connected to a slotted bar and a pin pushed through. The driver would give the bell code to the fireman on the footplate who would reply to the driver in the compartment. The driver worked the regulator on the locomotive with compressed air and also the vacuum brake from the driving compartment. From Seaton Junction to Seaton the locomotive would push the train in, running bunker first. From Seaton to Seaton Junction the locomotive would pull the train out.

HIGH DAYS & EVENTS

Interested spectators gathered on the platform at Sidmouth station, 7 March 1965. They were waiting to see the departure of GWR pannier tank no. 4666 with its three-coach train which had been chartered by the Locomotive Club of Great Britain for an East Devon rail tour.

In the sidings at Axminster station after the naming ceremony of the West Country class 21c118 *Axminster*, 25 June 1946. The members of Axminster station staff sitting on the locomotive are, left to right: porter Ben Hoskins, leading porter Don Matthews, porter Tom Jeffries, shunter Banger Boyle, booking clerk John Cannon, goods porter Fred Cook.

Miss Shepperd played a prominent part in the naming of the main line West Country class Pacific locomotive *Axminster*, 25 June 1946.

Colyford station, 8 July 1957. Pride of achievement is reflected in the faces of the Seaton branch permanent way staff who have just received a plaque for the best kept length. Left to right: John Seagar, lengthman; Charlie Cannings, inspector; Tom White, ganger; Mr Moore, the assistant chief engineer; the chief engineer from Exeter presenting the plaque; and Cyril Welch, lengthman.

Members of the Seaton branch line staff of the permanent way department assemble to receive a plaque for the best kept length, 29 June 1955. Left to right: Charlie Cannings, inspector; John Seagar, lengthman; Cyril Welch, lengthman; Mr Moore, assistant chief engineer; Tom White, ganger; the chief engineer from Exeter.

The last day of operation on the Lyme Regis branch line was 29 November 1965. Enthusiasts, many dressed in period Edwardian costume, gathered for the wake. Seen here at Axminster station, front row, left to right, are a guard from Exeter, the Lyme Regis Mayor, Tom Woodman, the train driver from Lyme Regis, Donald Baker, and Vincent Martyn.

Another picture taken on the last day of operation of the Lyme Regis branch line. The line opened on 24 August 1903, the first trains being hauled by Terriers no. 734 and no. 735. It served the community well but was regrettably 'axed' as a result of the Beeching Report in 1963.

Men from Honiton leaving by special train, August 1914. War fever swept Britain like an epidemic and people could hardly wait to get to grips with the Germans. They left Honiton station with those they left behind cheering, shouting, singing and waving goodbye with their handkerchiefs. It would be four long years before the war ended, and those that returned would find a country changed beyond recognition.

Following the night of 1 October 1960 when torrential rain caused severe flooding in the West Country there were more than thirty earth slips on Honiton incline, the 5 mile track between Seaton Junction and Honiton. With first light it was found that at three places rails were buried for stretches of 30 to 40 yds in 4 to 5 ft of mud. You can see this in the above picture which was taken at Snobs Corner, showing a caterpillar track excavator shovelling earth into empty wagons. In the picture below an S15 class engine and empty wagon cases pass the slips at Snobs Corner to wait for the excavator to load up the earth. Note the amount of water lying on the upside of the track.

In store at Exmouth Junction shed, standing in one of the little used roads behind the coal hopper, are Drummond 0–6–0 goods engines of the 700 class, nos 30689–30697 fitted with snow ploughs, 17 July 1962. In a few months time, following the blizzard of 27 December 1962, these engines would be in frequent use. There were no further snow falls to rival the one of 27 December but arctic conditions remained throughout January and February 1963, making this the most severe winter since 1740. It was during this winter, when the snow remained for over sixty days, that these engines were used over the Plymouth line on Dartmoor. The enginemen who worked them gave them the name of 'Black Motors'.

Such a sight we will never see again. Southern railway officials, members of the council and the people of Exeter gathered on platform one at Exeter Central station, 10 July 1945. The Second World War had just finished, and many ambitious schemes were to figure in post war development on the railways. The West Country class Pacifics were named after towns and cities in the west, and this is the naming ceremony of West Country class 4–6–2 Pacific no. 21c101 *Exeter*.

Sidmouth stationmaster Charles Greening is pictured here with staff members at his retirement ceremony in June 1952. He started work as stationmaster in 1936 and was held in high esteem by all who knew him. Mr Greening is seen receiving a gift of a table lamp, with his wife Freda standing beside him holding a bouquet of flowers. Other staff members include Ted Edwards, Jim Letten, Les Reed, Dick Morton, Bob Williams, Owen Leverton, Courtney Summers, Eric Helling, Jack Turner, Mrs E. Wells and Mrs K. Powell.

The end of an era for Seaton station: this is the last train to leave before line closure, 5 March 1966. The diesel unit stands in number two platform with Seaton driver Harold Pope in the DMU doorway. Beside him on the platform left to right are Exmouth Junction driver Lionel Melluish, Exeter guard Tony Perry, Exmouth Junction second man Norman Squires and Exmouth Junction driver Harold Denman.

A sad day for Seaton. Following the Beeching plan the closure of the line was proposed and despite strong local objections was confirmed by the Minister of Transport, becoming effective on 5 March 1966. This historic notice advertises the last round trip after ninety-eight years of service.

Axminster station, *c.* 1955. Adams tank no. 30582 stands in the bay platform during filming of the Lyme Regis branch by BBC television. Standing on the platform are the driver George Johns and motive power superintendent Sam Smith from Exmouth Junction shed, with fireman Grenville Morgan on the footplate.

A group of members of staff from Exmouth Junction shed, 28 March 1963. They had assembled for a photograph with a Nigerian student who had just finished his instruction course, following his visit to England to learn about the British railway system. Left to right: Fred Purton, chief clerk; Phil Isaccs, water tester; Dick ?, clerk; Horace Moore, shed master; the Nigerian student; Edgar Snow, inspector; Sam Smith, inspector; Cecil Balment, roster clerk; Douglas Simmons, clerk; Gordon Tilley, clerk; Jack Tilley, supervisor; Albert Watts, driver. In the background stands rebuilt Merchant Navy class Pacific no. 35013 *Blue Funnel Certum Pete Finem* with a 5,000 gallon tender. The photograph gives some idea of the size of these huge locomotives which weighed 137 tons 6 cwt.

Colyford Gates, *c.* 1951. Godfrey Foot, the branch guard, has just closed the level crossing gates to allow the two-coach pull and push set no. 381 through the crossing. Guards finished regular duties on the branch line trains in 1954.

A chapter of errors caused this derailment at the down siding at Seaton Junction during November 1929. A steam breakdown crane from Exmouth Junction shed is seen here lifting N class 2–6–0 mixed traffic engine no. 1829 which went over the bank during shunting duties. Apparently the engine went up the dead end siding instead of out on to the main line and was unable to stop. The shunter gave the signalman the wrong bell; the signalman pulled the wrong points; and the engine crew didn't check the ground signal before moving the engine.

The locomotive *Seaton* was a Light Pacific of the West Country class, no. 21c120. The naming ceremony on 25 June 1946 took place at Seaton Junction and was attended by members of Southern Railway and Seaton Urban District Council. In 1968 the name plate was presented by British Rail to the Seaton Urban District Council. The council failed to appreciate its great monetary and historical value, and through downright carelessness managed to lose it. Bearing in mind the size this must have been quite difficult to do!

Under the keen eye of stationmaster Colin Smith, Standard class tanks no. 41206 and no. 41308 from Exmouth Junction shed are seen here at Seaton Junction, 20 September 1964. They had just completed an SCTS Farewell to Steam rail tour of the Seaton branch line. The two engines are being uncoupled to run around the train and will then head off for either the Lyme Regis or the Yeovil Branch line for another tour.

EXMOUTH JUNCTION SHED

Exmouth Junction shed, 5 July 1957. Approximately 140 locomotives were allocated to Exmouth Junction shed, with over 400 men employed to attend to their needs. The shed, ¾ mile up the line from Exeter Central, was a busy place during the peak summer months, especially on a Saturday when the two disposal roads and the coaling plant would be full up. The shed was finally closed on 6 March 1967. In this picture, taken on a busy day in July, are, left to right, S15 class no. 30844 and no. 30841, Standard class 3 no. 82018, Battle of Britain class no. 34069 Hawkinge, a couple of unknown tanks, West Country class Camelford, and Drummond T9 no. 30712.

Exmouth Junction shed, 1962. Battle of Britain class no. 34057 *Biggin Hill* keeps company with S15 class no. 30844. The total number of locomotives in the West Country and Battle of Britain classes were 110, numbering 34001 to 34110.

Exmouth Junction shed, *c.* 1951. An unrebuilt Merchant Navy on shed, displaying the Devon Belle headboard, keeps company with West Country class no. 34021 *Dartmoor*.

Exmouth Junction old shed, 18 July 1925. Exmouth Junction shed seen here came into use during November 1887. The shed had approximately eleven roads, a 55 ft turntable and, north of the shed, two elevated coaling stages. Owing to unsuitable construction this shed was replaced during the 1920s. The locomotives on shed in this photograph were Adams 4–4–2 tank no. 69 of the 415 class and Adams 02 class 0–4–0 tank no. 228.

Exmouth Junction shed is pictured here in 1929 after rebuilding. On shed, left to right, are Drummond T9 class no. 703 4–4–0 King Arthur class, King Arthur class no. 449 *Sir Torre*, S15 class no. 824 and an unidentified N ORU class 2–6–0 in the outside road.

Adams tank no. 4–4–0 of the 380 class no. 162 (ex-no. 388) with Drummond chimney and round look-out windows, in an evocative picture taken at Exmouth Junction shed, 19 July 1924.

Drummond T9 class no. 710 looking very smart after being polished up by the cleaners. It was caught on camera at Exmouth Junction shed, 4 August 1928.

Exmouth Junction shed, 15 September 1963. Unrebuilt West Country class no. 34106 *Lydford* waits on shed with two 'Woolworths', one unidentified and the other no. 31812.

West Country class no. 34033 *Chard*, Exmouth Junction shed, 12 September 1964. 34033 was one of the few local engines in this class that never had a naming ceremony.

ACKNOWLEDGEMENTS

We are grateful to all those who have helped in the compilation of this book by contributing valuable information.

Michael would particularly like to thank many of his old railway colleagues who have given him so much of their time in recalling the details of days now long gone and for the loan of photographs. Special thanks must go to Ralph Bartlett and George Lawrence of Exeter for their time and help in giving assistance with information about Exmouth Junction shed. We are indebted to the photographers, both amateur and professional, whose pictures illustrate this book visually capturing the age of steam. They include: H.C. and R.M. Casserley, R.C. Riley, P.J. Lynch, Roger Joanes, Colin Caddy, Peter Barnfield, W.L. Underley, J.R. Besley, A.E. West, H.B. Priestley, Derek Cross, Ivor Peters, Gerald Sivior and the National Railway Museum.

We are also grateful to our wives Doris and Carol for their encouragement, and to Chellie Todd for her assistance with the compilation of the book. We would like to thank Simon Fletcher of Sutton Publishing for his assistance.

Most of the pictures in this book come from the superb collection of photographs belonging to Michael Clement. He would like to thank leading porter Ralph Watkins of Lyme Regis who, after taking a staff photograph in 1961 which included Michael, was the inspiration for his railway collection.

Ted Gosling
Michael Clement

For ninety-eight years thousands of passengers used the branch line at Seaton. Excited holidaymakers arrived and left, people travelled to and fro from work, businessmen left for appointments, and men from Seaton and Colyford went off to war. Year after year the pageant swept in some fresh form along the metalled track until that sad day when a great silence fell upon the line. Here we see Seaton station pictured a few years after the 1966 closure.